Kind of the...

Please excuse this... it's kinda amusing. It's kinda lame too... we have to put copyright info in and we weren't even allowed to have a drink when we wrote it... just skip it and go to the next page... it's much more amusing. There is even nudity to follow... but only in tasteful quantities. All facts and figures in this book were probably made up. This text is small for a reason.

© Copyright Eric Zork Alan. All rights reserved
ISBN: 0-9724111-5-1
Cover art and internal illustrations
© 2003, Eric Zork Alan

Alliterative Authors Press
21 Branch Brook Rd./ Suite 201
White Plains, NY 10605
beerbook@stolensnapshots.com

www.stolensnapshots.com

Origin of "99 bottles of beer"

It's a complete crock...there is NO origin to this song. It came out of the thin blue drunken air. Hours of research have left me with only a horrible headache and a need for 101 bottles of beer. Much complete bogus crap can be found about a 2,200 year old sailor/warrior song, computer code cryptograms, the "Ten Green Bottles" variation, and a 14th century poetry manuscript along with rumors of lost verses. I can't believe I spent hours researching this crap.

So, please, have a couple dozen drinks and don't you dare start singing this song!

[And isn't it a bit perverse that we are taught this song at age 9, while on a school bus to summer camp?]

"Beer is proof that god loves us and wants us to be happy."
-- Benjamin Franklin

"I have taken more out of alcohol than alcohol has taken out of me."
-- Winston Churchill

"He was a wise man who invented beer."
-- Plato

"It is disgusting to note the increase in the quantity of coffee used by my subjects and the amount of money that goes out of the country in consequence. Everybody is using coffee. If possible, this must be prevented. My people must drink beer."
-- Frederick the Great

Pints and Politics

Early politicians were fans of the flavor of beer. And when we started our little fight with the Brits it caused a small problem because they supplied much of our beer. So Tom Jefferson passed legislation to promote the settlers' paths of brewing beers.

The first microbrewery was developed by the Dutch in New Amsterdam [later called NYC] in the early 1600s. The 1800s saw a couple thousand microbeweries. But then, for some silly reason, Jan 16, 1920 saw the start of prohibition [enter Al C. & Elliot N.] that lasted until Dec 5, 1933 when FDR had the sense to stop that 18th Amendment nonsense.

In 1987 homebrewing was legalized on a national level. God bless America and Jimmy Carter.

(For a low-fat diet, beer is better than milk)

Beer Breakfast

While DRINKING beer for breakfast is a bad, bad thing that only a drunk would do, it is perfectly acceptable to pour pints into pourage or supplement cereal. For a properly balanced breakfast, add beer to a fortified cereal and be light on the sugar.

Advantages
- doesn't sour like milk
- loaded with nutritious barley and hops
- can use LIGHT beer for dietary needs
- can help make raw pasta a good breakfast [high in fiber too]
- get's the day off to a shiny [and sometimes sloppy] start

Disadvantages
- well, you will get to work drunk, and then be promptly fired [there are trade-offs to everything in life]

George Washington's Recipe for Beer

[hand written note from 1757 notebook available for viewing at the New York Public Library]

To make Small Beer

Take a large Sifter full of Bran Hops to your Taste -- Boil these 3 hours. Then strain out 30 Gall. into a Cooler put in 3 Gallons Molasses while the Beer is scalding hot or rather drain the molasses into the Cooler. Strain the Beer on it while boiling hot let this stand til it is little more than Blood warm. Then put in a quart of Yeast if the weather is very cold cover it over with a Blanket. Let it work in the Cooler 24 hours then put it into the Cask. leave the Bung open til it is almost done working -- Bottle it that day Week it was Brewed.

[beer ingrediants: water, malted barley, hops, yeast + special stuff]

Beer Brewing Basics

- **Making the Malt (bring out the barley)**: in this **soak and short sprout stage**, water is added and the starch starts to become sugar (mostly maltose). Then it all must dry before the batch is brewable.
- **Make the Mash (for what it's WORT):** combine the malt and other special flavor ingredients (raspberry, coffee, spices etc.) with hot water to make the mash... this liquid sugar stuff is called "wort"
- **Boil the Brew** for 30-90 minutes and add hops (makes beer bitter) & "special stuff" to the mix. This is finely filtered.
- **Fantastic Fermentation [or yuck it's yeast]:** After 48 hours of natural fireworks, this is basically the boring part where plenty of patience is the main ingredient. The wort is cooled, yeast is added and the whole concoction ferments for 10 days to 8 weeks depending on the yeast chosen and desired results. Since this all takes quite some time you should stock up on store bought six packs first.

For a kit to brew your own beer go to:
www.stolensnapshots.com/beerkits.html

A pickup poem

Did I get that right?

when I caught you catching me
catching your eye?

Your paused, perched, posed
… *perfectly*

**Did I get that right when I brushed by you
on way to nowhere
but by you?**

Did I get it right?

By the by, I couldn't help but catch you
catch my eye.

Did I get that right?

Spare Parts

It is a little known fact that beer bottles are made of sand. Considering the remarkable conversion it made into beer bottles, it only makes sense that beer bottles could be useful in many other ways.

While furniture parts may be a stretch, if you diet a lot and switch to light beer there is no reason to rule it out.

Sand does NOT conduct electricity so beer bottles can NOT be used for spare spark plugs. One can only expect so much from sand.

I think I'll have a drink now
[08/05/02 @ 4:09pm]

I can sleep late
dream another dream

like that one last week
where I imagined
waking up
mattered for much

I think I'll have a drink now
maybe two or three

till I forget work tomorrow

Do you really think
anyone will notice?

I'll let Peter get the last cup of coffee
And Sue *something-or-another*
can bring the donuts

Will "Will" whats-his-name,
that boss guy,
even notice if
I don't show?

I think I'll have
a drink now
and sing myself a lullaby
right here in my chair

Staring at the wall
I start to see spots

[sip]

tiny spots

[sip, sip]

so many spots

I can sleep late now

Beer Garden

Advantages

- consistent bloom
- beer kept naturally cold in winter
- saves mini fridge space
- always spare stock of beer... outside
- sobrierty [because garden looks too damn good to drink]
- minimal maintence [never needs to be watered]
- less aftertaste than daisies
- be the 1st on the block

Hey, pumpkins can like pints too
They're people too...or so this pum*King* told me
after I bought him a few beers

Observing Oktoberfest

The world's largest annual festival started in 1810 when Prince Ludwig of Bavaria [later to be King Ludwig I] wanted the people of his public [as opposed to the hermits] to share in his marital bliss in a two week long drunken celebration.

Ludwig and Princess Therese von Sachen-Hildburghausen were wed on October 12, 1810.

With about 30,000 guests [of a total Munich population of about 40,000] this party probably cost a pretty penny for this politician, but I am sure he made up for it with taxes and maybe even thought of making people pay for public executions.

Since there are now over 6 million people at Oktoberfest there is no longer an open bar.

"Oktoberfest, USA" became a Wisconsin tradition in 1961.

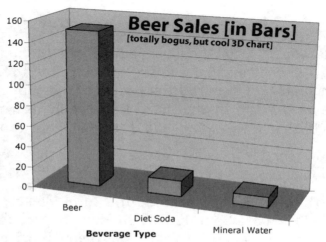

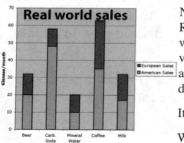

Notice how tough this small REAL boring chart is to read. I was a bit tipsy when I did the survey above... but it should be accurate (give or take 5 or 6 standard devations [or beers]).

It is a pretty 3D chart, though.

What would your chart look like?

people buy beer (when in bars)

As the absurdly pointless [and completely poorly researched] chart on the left shows, beer sells in surprising quantities compared to mineral water and Diet Soda. It should be overlooked that this study was conducted at biased bars where bikers and beer drinkers were not too likely to be ordering mineral water or diet soda because their girlfriends would then call them sissys and have the stud on the next stool buy them a blow job or a slippery nipple.

So, the moral of the story is, when in a bar... buy beer... it MUST be better.

Contrary to popular myth, the *real* blarney stone lives comfortably on the author's kitchen floor. Taking the tradition of kissing the blarney stone a bit too seriously, he "makes out" with it on a regular basis... and you can see where *that* habit got him.

Sláinte/Cultural "Cheers"

"Sláinte" pronounced "sloynta" means "cheers" in Irish [Gaelic]

At Irish pubs, along with a good fake accent, you might get a couple freebies if you pretend to be from the homeland. Be sure to tell your made up story about kissing the "blarney stone" as a child...bring a fake photo.

After your pint is poured thank your bartender by saying "Go raibh maith agat." And if, during the course of the evening, your pants catch on fire it will help to say "Tá mo bhriste trí thine."

Saving (up for) St. Patty's Day

If you were born Maewyn Succat and sold into slavery at the age of 16 wouldn't you want to get a clean start and change your name to Saint Patrick? Born in 387 A.D., after the stint of slavery and escaping to a British monastery (where they all were considerably nicer) he was sent to Ireland in 432 A.D. to convert the pagans to the Christian cross.

Here he worked for 30 years doing such things as "driving all the snakes from Ireland"... only, since there were NO SNAKES in Ireland, one must surmise that it was a metaphor for driving all the pagans out. You'd have to ask a poet to be sure about the metaphor [this author just writes beer books].

St. Patty's day has long been associated with the three-leaved shamrock. This was a clever teacher's metaphor to explain the concept of the Holy Trinity. Three leafs are a part of one whole clover... just as the Father, Son and Holy Ghost are considered the 3 parts of the Catholic trinity.

Saint Patrick is said to have died on March 17th, 461 A.D., but some say there was an argument that he died on the 8th or the 9th, so they just added the disputed dates.

St. Patrick's day first was celebrated in the US in 1737 in Boston.

But, back then in Beantown, the bars were probably STILL closing at 2 a.m.

Beer Bath

Beer has long been known to be good as a shampoo supplement to create a shiny head of hair.

So, if you want to be super sexy, be good to your WHOLE body with a beer bath. While a bit costly, every once in a while you should spoil yourself.

For those special dates try an imported beer bath... after you have been going steady you can switch to PBR.

Type of Beer	$/Gallon	Total $
Imported	$13.77	$578
American	$7.40	$311
P.B.R.	$4.88	$205
*cost presuming 42 gallon bath. Add approx. 32% for Jacuzzi.		

Barkeep caters his own Funeral

Babe, a bar owner in Yonkers, New York prepared the party for his own wake.

He has just finished prepping a Super-Bowl party at his bar when he died. So, quite conveniently, there was plenty of food and drink for his funeral friends.

Babe's bar was the last bar in Westchester, NY to sell nickel beers and also sold "beer to go" in a cardboard carton.

Those were the days!

Shot Senseless

- **Slippery Nipple** [also a Camel Hump]
[Bailey's Irish Cream, Butterscotch schnapps]
[add Cherry liqueur for a "Buttery nipple with a cherry kiss"]
[add Midori melon liqueur for an "Alien Nipple"]
[add Goldschlager and a dash of 151 rum for a "Branded Nipple"]

- **Cum shot**
[Vodka, Peach schnapps, Kumquat]
[or add whipped cream to a "Slippery Nipple"]

- **Blow Job**
[Kahlua, Bailey's irish cream, whipped cream]

- **Flaming Blow Job**
[Jack Daniels, Everclear, chocolate milk, whipped cream]

- **Lemon Drop**
[vodka, lemon, sugar on rim]

- **Shot-o-Happiness**
[Goldschlager, Razzmatazz, Pineapple juice, Sweet & Sour, 7-up]

- **Cockteaser** [antithesis of "Shot-o-happiness"]
[Triple sec, Peach schnapps, Midori Melon Liqueur]

- **Body Shot** [involves lots of lime and licking]
[find someone REALLY hot (and hopefully horny) and ask them to show you... or offer to teach them... learning can be fun]

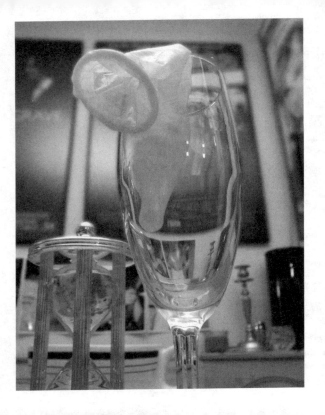

Drinks with smutty names

- ## Sex on the beach
[grapefruit & cranberry juice, 3/4oz Peach Schnapps, 1oz vodka]
- ## Sex on my face
[Yukon Jack, Mailbu Rum, Southern Comfort, Banana Liquer (.5 oz each), splashes of Cranberry, Pineapple & Orange juice]
- ## Sex appeal [aka the drink everyone wants]
[White Rum, Coconut Rum, Melon Liquer, Peach Schnapps, Blue Curacao (.5 oz all), Sour Mix, splash lemonade, lemon slice]
- ## Screaming Orgasm [the drink everyone REALLY wants]
[1 oz Vodka, 1.5oz Bailey's Irish Cream .5oz Kahlua]
- ## Screaming Multiple Climax
[White Cream de Cacao, Ameretto, Frangelico Hazelnut Liqueur, Cream de Banane (.5oz each), 1 oz. vodka, fill with cream]
- ## A Piece of Ass
[sour mix, ice cubes, Southern Comfort, Amaretto]
- ## Asbolut Royal Fuck
[splash Pineapple & Cranberry juice, .5 oz Peach Schnapps, .5 oz Absolut Kurant, 1 oz Crown Royal]
- ## Screw Up [if you don't get any sex(drinks) have a Screw Up]
[1 part vodka, 1 part OJ, 4 parts 7-Up]

Drinking Games

- ## Quarters
(bounce a quarter into a shot glass, then make someone drink... after 3 successful shots in a row you start to make really silly rules... this is the game responsible for the author now being called "ZORK") [chandeliers is a spin off with a circle of glasses]

- ## Truth or Dare
(a documentary film that showcased this game... Madonna's true love is Sean... don't play this game when you are ALREADY in a relationship)

- ## Mexican
(somehow involves dice, a cup, and drinks... play one of the other games instead)

- ## Spin the bottle
(spin the bottle and then start stripping... I am not sure where the drinking is required...but it sure helps... this is the best game of the bunch)

- ## Strip Poker
(again no drinking necesary, but hard to imagine playing without proper amounts of alchohol)

- ## Asshole, Cups, Up & Down the River
[check out www.stolensnapshots.com for the proper descriptions of these games gunaranteed to give you a hang over and cost you much "morning after" embarrassment]

Burroughs' Beer

William Burroughs, author of "Naked Lunch", may have been an influential writer, but he had a tendency to work under the influence of substances far more serious that bottled beer.

Sometimes for fun he would test his marksmanship by doing a "William Tell Act" under the influence of various substances.

But, in 1951 after killing his wife Joan by trying to shoot a highball glass off her head at a 6' range , he probably regretted that he didn't use a beer bottle instead which would have been taller.

William was in Mexico City where killing loved ones is less illegal than in the United States and only consutitutes a $2,312 fine and about $2k in legal fees. DO NOT try this at home or at your local pub. It won't be funny.

People used to poison pints

Beware of beer clinkers: A frightening fact to toast to is that the glass clinking ritual of toasting overflowing beer mugs was to make sure you weren't being poisoned by your drinking buddies.

You see if YOUR drink was poisoned [by your supposed buddy] he would get poisoned from the overflowing ale that would splash into HIS mug.

Be wary of your friend and ALWAYS toast with a hard clink.

Better drunk than dead

Origin of beer

Wine probably came first and actually from a princely poison, but beer was a close 2nd. Many experts agree that it goes back to about 10,000 B.C. in Mesoppotamia and Sumer. Beer may have been accidentally discovered trying to bake bread [they share many common ingredients]. Barley is considered to be the first grain grown [and normally what makes beer], but early forms of beer are also based on corn [or whatever was convenient]. Egyptians and the Chinese are also early creators. As to the states, Native American's offered beer to the settlers and they got hooked.

This is NOT really Ninkasi... she would be much older now... about 4,000 years older... but this chick sure is cute!
I would have written her a poem AND built her a keg for her beer

Ninkasi: Goddess of Beer

Several sources say that the oldest known written recipe is a formula for beer that is part of an epic 19th Century B.C. poem "The Hymn to Ninkasi" devoted to Ninkasi, the Sumerian goddess of beer.

The poem was written some 4,000 years ago on a clay cuneiform tablet.

"You are the one who holds with both hands the great sweet wort,
Brewing [it] with honey and wine
(You the sweet wort to the vessel)
Ninkasi"
-- [translation by Miguel Civil]

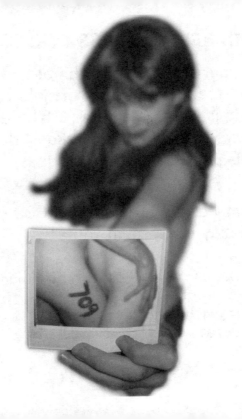

Private Polaroids

At a friend's birthday party
I met you
after you were talking to another guy

I take a private Polaroid of you and him,
scratch him out,
paste myself in instead

It makes a better picture

It's perfectly clear
I'll show you later,
take a new Polaroid

A little later at the bar,
where we both have had 1
or 4
too many shots
I break convention,
focus on first kiss,

[I take a private Polaroid]

The lesson of the lime

Here's another one with a debatable origin [drunk people aren't very good and documenting the facts]. Some say that limes [and lemons] were used to wipe the rim of reused bottles to kill the beer bottle bacteria. One report elaborated that tough guys would then poke the dirty lime in the bottle and drink it to prove just how tough they are. [If this sounds unbelievable, just think of the worm]. Others say that the lime keeps the flies away [if only it kept BAR-flies away]. My Mexican friend says... "the lime tastes good! That's that". Bottom line is some marketing genius is a genius for making us all go along with the great gimmick.

BeerVlogs.com

Eric ZORK Alan & Sweetie

Professional Poets / Beer Vloggers

zork@mac-tune-up.com
Local Bar Near You
Anytown, AnyState, 00000

www.youtube.com/iamnotapoet

things to do with beer bottles
[07/29/02 @ 8:14pm]

first
launch the lime down her neck
force finger down shaft
tip her upside down
and poke it in hard
swirl it around
swing upright
and swig
take a second and
appreciate her taste
now that you have her attention
it is time to be more creative
and show her
the 69 nine other things you can do
with beer bottles

Don't drive drunk

How drunk will you be tonight? [Blood alcohol levels to heed]

"Hey, why is your smile upside down now? You were rightside up just 2 or 3 drinks ago."

- 6 beers/hour
- 5 beers/hour
- 4 beers/hour
- 3 beers/hour
- 2 beers/hour
- 1 beer/hour

Weight: 100lb Female, 100lb Male, 140lb Female, 140lb Male, 180lb Female, 180lb Male, 220lb Female, 220lb Male

In most states a level exceeding .08 or .10 is "legally drunk." So if you are lucky enough to be 220 lbs you can drink 5 beers an hour and only sort of go to jail. It does sometimes benefit to be "big boned"... but it always pays to stay sober.

52 Pickup

Here are a couple of pages of REALLY bad pickup lines... matching a deck of cards you can buy separately. If any of them work, then it is most likely that you happen to look like Johnny Depp and the women are just forgiving your stupidity. If, on the much more likely event, you get slapped, then just have another drink.

Joker
U would be
Joking
If you said "no"
when it is all too clear
you want me so

2 of diamonds
2 me u r a diamond
in the ruff...
ain't nothing a little
buffing can't make better

3 of diamonds
THREEmendously excited
I am about taking you home
to shine... shine u
delicious diamond

4 of diamonds
4 one day soon
u will prove me
much more than glass

5 of diamonds

In 5 minutes
u will be mine
but only if you
cut me some slack

6 of diamonds

let's keep it simple
skip the sex
and cuddle

7 of diamonds

and on the 7th
day
God made u shine

8 of diamonds

I ache in
more than 8
ways to find *all* your
facets

9 of diamonds

it's your matrix
that makes me
make this move

10 of diamonds

I'm the man holding the
cards
can I count you in?

Jack of diamonds

U know
it is so damn rough
for me to keep pretending
I am quite this tough

Queen of hearts

Can you be my queen of
hearts?

King of diamonds
In my kingdom
I will make sure you
shine

Ace of hearts
Can't you see
I am not the ace of spades?

Ace of hearts
In the Ace of hearts
u will find a home
[tonight and maybe even still
tomorrow morning]

2 of hearts
2-day let's
hold on,
hear everything,
harmonize a tune or 2
and maybe
hump

3 of hearts
Would a 3-some
on a heart-shaped bed
in the Pocanos pose
a problem 4 u?

4 of hearts
4 play is

my favorite form of fun

5 of clubs
would u be
the 5th fling
in my carnal club?

the editor apologizes for the worst imaginable collection of pick-up lines. Email less stupid ones to pickuplines@stolensnapshots.com

Things to say (or do) to idiots using the pickup line on previous page

- Isn't it about 10,000 years away from the twelfth of never?

- I would, indeed, let you buy me a drink if only I had no standards and then set them lower still.

- Are you well aware of the protocols and mating rituals of the praying mantis? And, hmm, you do look quite yummy!

- Please stay away from stupid beer books!

- DO NOT physically assault the man. We are living in a new millennium, and there are many women that can beat men's butts... but men CAN sue you. So insult instead. Let them buy you a drink and then loudly insult the size of their penis [do NOT verify the slanderous statements... you may sometimes be right (or wrong)]

See no evil: DO NOT read this page

- Alchohol can cause cancer
- Strokes are serious stuff
- short term and long term memory can become impaired
- You WILL get fatter
- Impotence is inconvenient
- You may not get hard, but if you drink a 6 pack at a time your arteries will
- DWI = go to jail, do not collect $200

P.S. I TOLD you you didn't want to read this page

telegram

```
need to write poem [stop]
at loss 4 words [stop]
[and] have lost all pencils [stop]
do u remember [stop]
how 2 jump start me? [stop]
remember once u
taught me some trick [stop]
involving salt, lime, liquor and lips [stop]
possibly [short] shot glass and
carefully cupped cleavage
were involved [stop]
can't remember proof [stop]
of spirits [stop]
it seemed to work then [stop]
revitalized writing [stop]
lost [forgot] recipe [stop]
please send self in [return] addressed
postage paid envelope [stop]
enclose sharpened # 2 [stop]
then [[stop]]
don't [stop]
```

* excerpted from *"Stolen Snapshots: I am not a poet"*

www.stolensnapshots.com

From the acclaimed author of the "Push Up Poem" and "Things to do with Beer Bottles"

over 10,000 copies in print
Foreword by Drift Away's Dobie Gray
Backword by Manhunter's Tom Noonan
Monkee on my back [Davy Jones blurb]

Stolen Snapshots: I am NOT a poet
poetry (of sorts) by Eric Zork Alan

"If Ronnie Spector married Bob Dylan, their child would be somewhat like Zork: able to translate desire."

It should be no small surprise that there are twice as many Beer Books in print as Zork's poetry book.

Shameless Plug for not-so-foo-foo poetry book

Hard as it may be to imagine, the author of this book writes performance poetry. You may think it's stupid and kind of a sissy thing... but I am sure you will score big points from your girlfriend for buying her the book. And, if you are a girl, then please showcase your poetic patronage and support a stranger with his artistic endeavors.

To all, fear not, I don't do rotten rhymes, but I alliterate like a bastard.

See order info on opposite page.

Davy Jones, a marvelous Monkee, said: "if you buy a book and it's not mine, buy this"

Order Page

To order more of these silly books to give away at beer bashes, frat parties, and as VERY "CHEAP" gifts to your friends ask you local book store or visit amazon.com or bn.com.

This book is available by the six pack and case on www.stolensnapshots.com. There you will also find foo-foo books of poetry and mugs that say "I am NOT a poet"...
because we know you are.

Email Zork beer info/trivia/stories to:
beerinfo@stolensnapshots.com
www.stolensnapshots.com